It's I!

Mary Elizabeth Salzmann

Consulting Editor, Diane Craig, M.A./Reading Specialist

Published by ABDO Publishing Company, 8000 West 78th Street, Edina, Minnesota 55439. Copyright © 2010 by Abdo Consulting Group, Inc. International copyrights reserved in all countries. No part of this book may be reproduced in any form without written permission from the publisher. Super SandCastle™ is a trademark and logo of ABDO Publishing Company.

Printed in the United States.

♻ PRINTED ON RECYCLED PAPER

Editor: Katherine Hengel
Content Developer: Nancy Tuminelly
Cover and Interior Design and Production: Kelly Doudna, Mighty Media
Photo Credits: iStockphoto (Jani Bryson), Photodisc, Shutterstock

Library of Congress Cataloging-in-Publication Data
Salzmann, Mary Elizabeth, 1968-
  It's I! / Mary Elizabeth Salzmann.
     p. cm. -- (It's the alphabet!)
  ISBN 978-1-60453-596-9
  1. English language--Alphabet--Juvenile literature. 2. Alphabet books--Juvenile literature. I. Title.
  PE1155.S267 2010
  421'.1--dc22
  〈E〉
                          2009020949

Super SandCastle™ books are created by a team of professional educators, reading specialists, and content developers around five essential components— phonemic awareness, phonics, vocabulary, text comprehension, and fluency—to assist young readers as they develop reading skills and strategies and increase their general knowledge. All books are written, reviewed, and leveled for guided reading, early reading intervention, and Accelerated Reader® programs for use in shared, guided, and independent reading and writing activities to support a balanced approach to literacy instruction.

About SUPER SANDCASTLE™

**Bigger Books for Emerging Readers
Grades K–4**

Created for library, classroom, and at-home use, Super SandCastle™ books support and engage young readers as they develop and build literacy skills and will increase their general knowledge about the world around them. Super SandCastle™ books are an extension of SandCastle™, the leading preK–3 imprint for emerging and beginning readers. Super SandCastle™ features a larger trim size for more reading fun.

Let Us Know
Super SandCastle™ would like to hear your stories about reading this book. What was your favorite page? Was there something hard that you needed help with? Share the ups and downs of learning to read. We want to hear from you! Send us an e-mail.

sandcastle@abdopublishing.com

Contact us for a complete list of SandCastle™, Super SandCastle™, and other nonfiction and fiction titles from ABDO Publishing Company.

www.abdopublishing.com • 8000 West 78th Street
Edina, MN 55439 • 800-800-1312 • 952-831-1632 fax

Aa Bb Cc Dd Ee
Ff Gg Hh Ii Jj Kk
Ll Mm Nn Oo Pp
Qq Rr Ss Tt Uu Vv
Ww Xx Yy Zz

The Letter Ii

The letter i in
American Sign Language

I and i
can also look like

Ii   **Ii**

Ii   Ii

Ii   Ii

4

The letter i is
a vowel.

It is the 9th
letter of the
alphabet.

short i as in s**i**x

ship

k**i**tten

6

Tim

Tim lives in his ship
with six little kittens.

☞ long i as in f**i**nd and n**i**ne

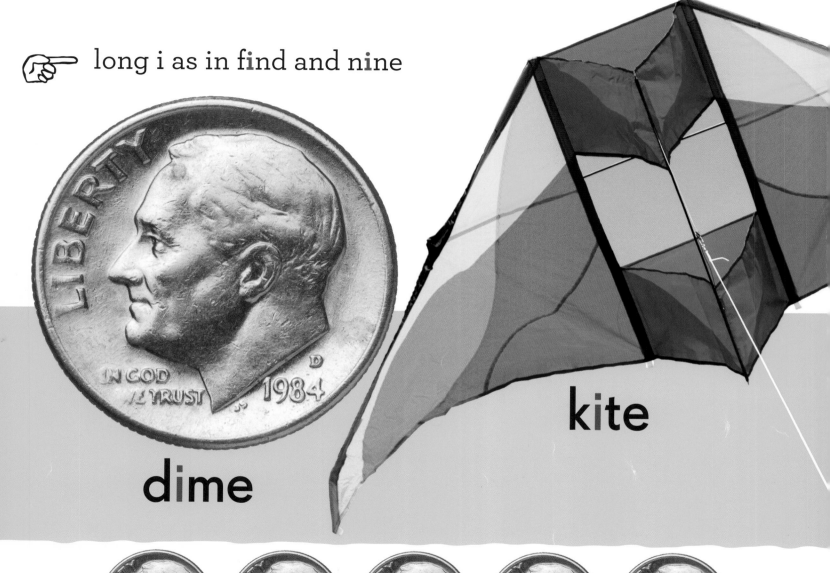

d**i**me

k**i**te

Mike

Mike says, "I can find a kite for the price of nine shiny dimes."

9

ir as in b**ir**thday

giraffe

shirt

Kirsten got a giraffe
and thirteen shirts
for her birthday.

Kirsten

pink

fingers

Lincoln is eating wings with his fingers and drinking something pink.

wings

ie as in tried

spies

ties

The spies wearing ties tried fried pies.

pies

13

Iris the builder lives on a tropical isle.

She likes shirts with flowers because they are in style.

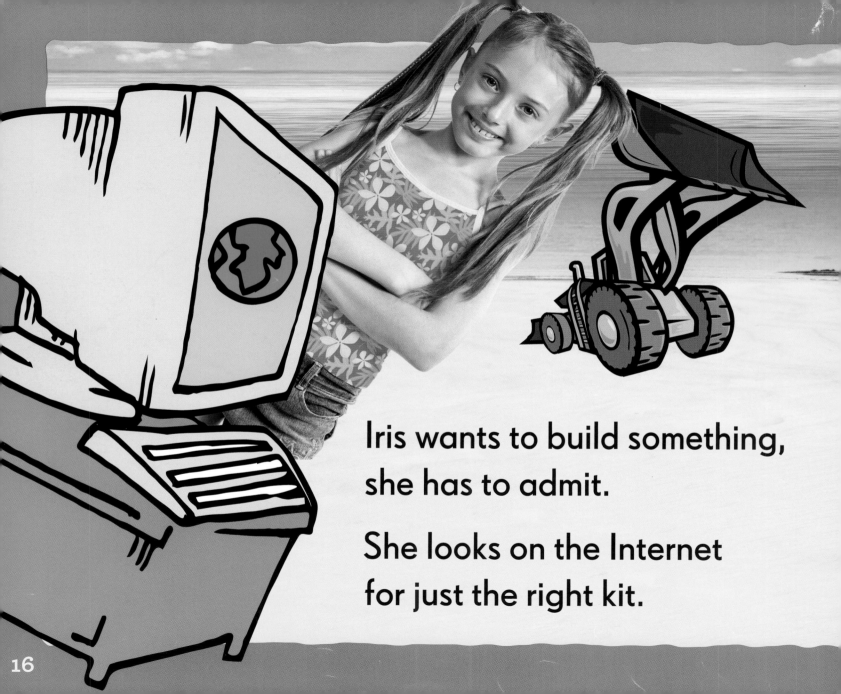

Iris wants to build something,
she has to admit.

She looks on the Internet
for just the right kit.

She spies an igloo kit with a price that is right.

Iris signs up to have it shipped in overnight.

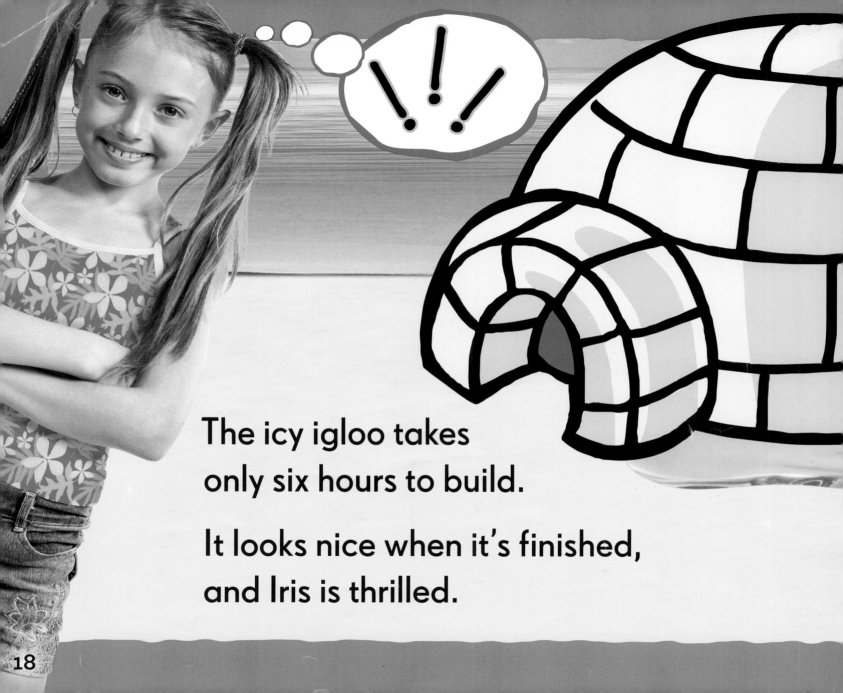

The icy igloo takes
only six hours to build.

It looks nice when it's finished,
and Iris is thrilled.

But soon the ice melts which disappoints Iris.

With hands on her hips she quips, "This is a crisis!"

Iris thinks for a bit
and comes up with a trick.

The next igloo she builds
will be made of red brick!

Which words have the
same **i** sound as h**i**s?

dime

ship   six   kitten

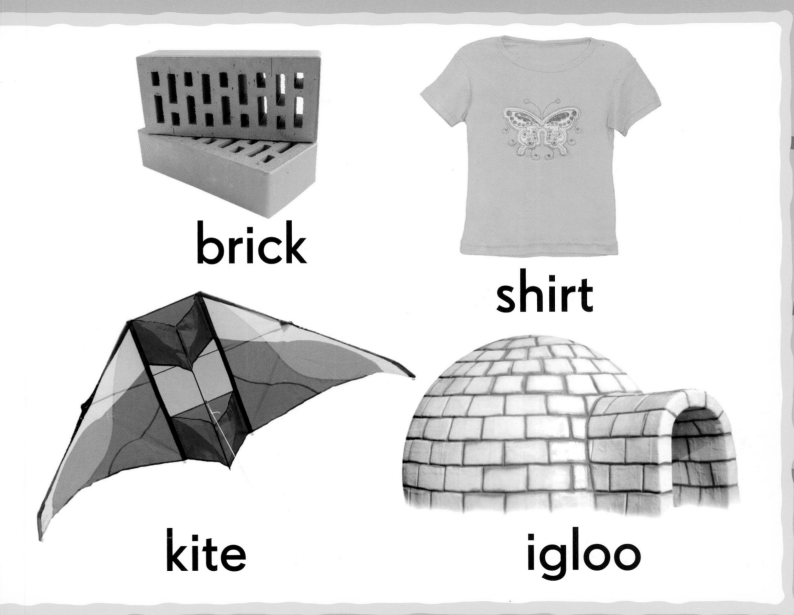

brick

shirt

kite

igloo

Glossary

admit (p. 16) – to say that something is so.

brick (pp. 20, 23) – a block of clay baked hard and used for building.

crisis (p. 19) – a bad or difficult situation.

disappoint (p. 19) – to make someone feel sad because something hoped for didn't happen.

igloo (pp. 17, 18, 20, 23) – a traditional dome-shaped house built by the Inuit people.

isle (p. 15) – a small island.

quip (p. 19) – to make a joke or funny statement.

spy (pp. 13, 17) – 1. a person who secretly watches what other people do. 2. to see or find.

thrill (p. 18) – to make someone feel very excited or happy.

tropical (p. 15) – located in one of the hottest areas on earth.

To promote letter recognition, letters are highlighted instead of glossary words in this series. The page numbers above indicate where the glossary words can be found.

More Words with I

Find the **i** in the beginning or middle of each word.

animal	hill	inch	iron	light
big	icon	indeed	island	lion
bring	idea	ink	itself	miss
dinosaur	ill	inside	ivy	quiet
drive	imagine	instead	kid	ride
guide	important	into	king	zipper